Comfort
for the
Grieving Soul

CAROLYN JANE NEILL

Printed by CreateSpace Independent Publishing Platform
An Amazon.com Company
Headquarters Seattle, Washington, United States

Copyright © 2015 Carolyn Jane Neill

All rights reserved. No part of this publication may be reproduced, stored in a retrieval system, or transmitted in any form or by any means, electronic, mechanical, photocopying, recording or otherwise, without the prior written permission of the author.

ISBN-10: 1499677464
ISBN-13: 978-1499677461

Available from Amazon.com and other retail outlets

In loving memory of...

My beautiful Mum Sally, who encouraged me to
"Follow your dreams and all your dreams will come true."

My Grandparents Don & Katherine, Eric & Nancy
"My love for you grows stronger each day."

CONTENTS

PROLOGUE	Page 1
DENIAL	Page 5
ANGER	Page 19
BARGAINING	Page 33
DEPRESSION	Page 49
ACCEPTANCE	Page 69
THE PRICELESS GIFT OF LIFE	Page 91
SPECIAL THANKS	Page 94

PROLOGUE

Coping with grief is a personal experience
that is unique to everyone it touches.

It's difficult for those yet to experience grief to understand the sudden
and profound effect it can have on one's life. More confusing, can be
how to support someone that is going through this challenging period.

This book is designed to comfort you through your individual journey
through grief and help you realise that what you are feeling is natural.

It may even make you smile...

There are five stages of grief
that you may experience.

Just when you think you've
made it through one stage
and you're progressing into another,
you may regress to the previous
stage or jump ahead.
It really is different for everyone.

Although it certainly won't feel
like it now, in time the intense emotion
and chaos that has become your life
will ease and a sense
of normality will return.

When this time comes, you will feel blessed
to have shared your life with your loved one.

And remember them with a warm smile,
as you carry them in your heart each and every day.

DENIAL

The **shock** you feel when hearing the news.

Your heart pounds and you're **breathless** too.

Time stands still and your legs **give way.**

Your mind races, becoming **foggier** each day.

Sure enough,
the **tears**
soon come.

For quite a while
you feel **sad and glum**.

Your mind is
so busy you
barely **sleep**.

Hunger has gone
and you hardly eat.

You may be **numb** and not feel a thing.

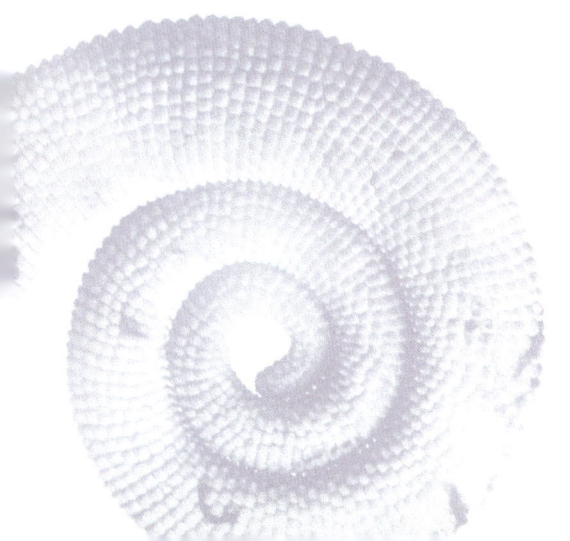

Your memory fades and you **forget** such little things.

You may **sense**
that your loved one
is still around.

This brings great **comfort**,
helping you settle down.

Denial is a very normal coping mechanism and must be recognized as performing a genuine role in initiating the grieving process. As a protective device, it is designed to buffer the system from the trauma of an event too tragic to deal with all at once.

Ronald J. Knapp, Beyond Endurance
Published by AuthorHouse, 2005.

ANGER

As the numbness passes you will feel **pain**.

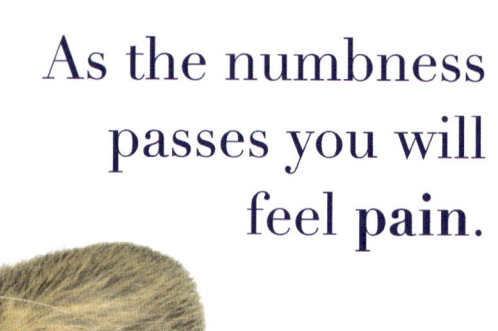

Just ride it through
for **relief** you will gain.

You may get **angry** and ask why.

And sure enough,
again and again
you will **cry**.

Be **kind** to yourself and don't expect too much.

Accomplishing one **task** a day is more than enough.

If you forget what your loved one looked like,
don't **freak out**.

It's quite **natural**
and you'll work it out.

Talking it through will help get your **feelings** out.

You may even feel like a **scream** or shout.

Hold on tight
as these
strange
feelings
will not last.

In time, they will all be in the **past**.

All emotions have their proper place in a man's life; the experience of emotion is what makes life rich. And there are times when anger is an appropriate reaction to events and people.

Thomas Harbin, Beyond Anger
Published by Da Capo Press, 2000.

BARGAINING

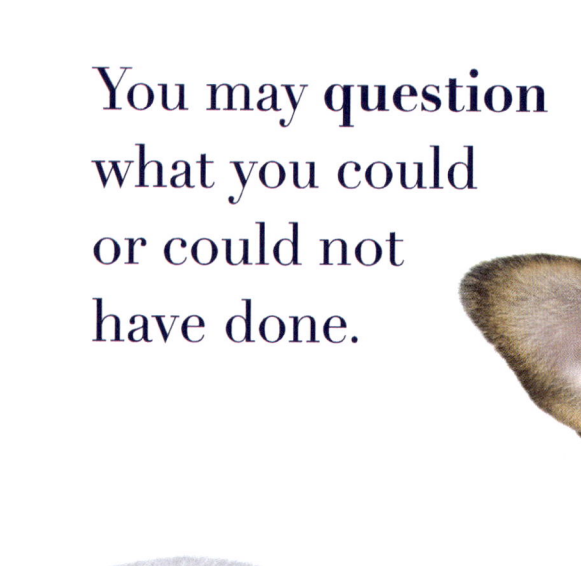

You may **question** what you could or could not have done.

Going down this path of **thinking** is not much fun.

Get **together** with your family and friends.

Company during this time will help you no end.

Instead of thinking
of the **'what ifs'**
of the past.

Live in the **present** moment as if it were your last.

If ever in doubt
a big **hug** will
certainly do.

Laughter is great medicine too.

Try and focus on **other people** as well.

This will help
ease you out
of your
shell.

Your family and
friends love you
and want
to **help**.

Make sure **you**
let them know
what they can do.

Maybe it's **shopping** or cooking a meal or two.

Keeping you **company** or regularly checking on you.

Face reality as it is, not as it was or as you wish it to be.

Jack Welch, retired business executive, author
and former chairman and CEO of General Electric.

DEPRESSION

Spending some time by **yourself** may help you work through your grief.

Asking others for **space** also gives them some relief.

Some days you may not want to **open** your eyes.

Other days you may
feel quite okay, which
is a welcomed **surprise**.

Following a normal **routine** can make you feel better too.

Keeping **busy** doing some
of your favourite things
will help you.

Head outside for some **exercise**.

It will make you feel more
energised.

Get together with
your favourite **bunch**.

Treat yourself to
a delicious lunch.

Soak in the **bath** for as long as you like.

Get some **fresh air** and have a push on a bike.

Massage is a great way
to **soothe** the soul.

It will help
your heart
mend its hole.

Be **thankful** for the time that you shared.

Focus your energy
on those for whom
you care.

If you need help,
make sure you **reach out**.

Support is available,
there's no need to miss out.

When you're in a slump, you're not in for much fun.
Un-slumping yourself is not easily done.

Dr Seuss, Oh, the Places You'll Go!
Published by Random House, 1990.

ACCEPTANCE

Saying **goodbye** is certainly the hardest part.

Realising you won't see
or speak to them again
can **break** your heart.

It is not **expected** that we then fill their shoes.

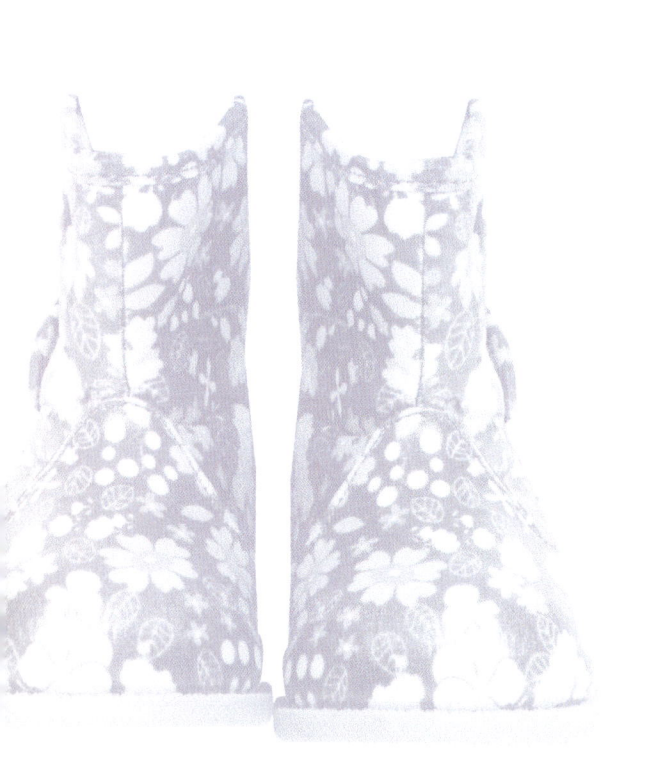

By mistakenly doing this,
ourself we will **lose**.

The dynamic of your relationships may **change**.

By simply **accepting** this
you will avoid unnecessary pain.

You may experience something new and **excitedly** reach for the phone.

Then remembering they've gone, you feel **sad and alone**.

Express your feelings however you see fit.

Simply talking
to them
or writing a letter
you will **benefit**.

Give your loved one the send off that they so **deserve.**

Celebrate their life and achievements without reserve.

You will find your own **special** way.

To **honour** the memory
of your loved one
each day.

With patience and time you will begin to **heal**.

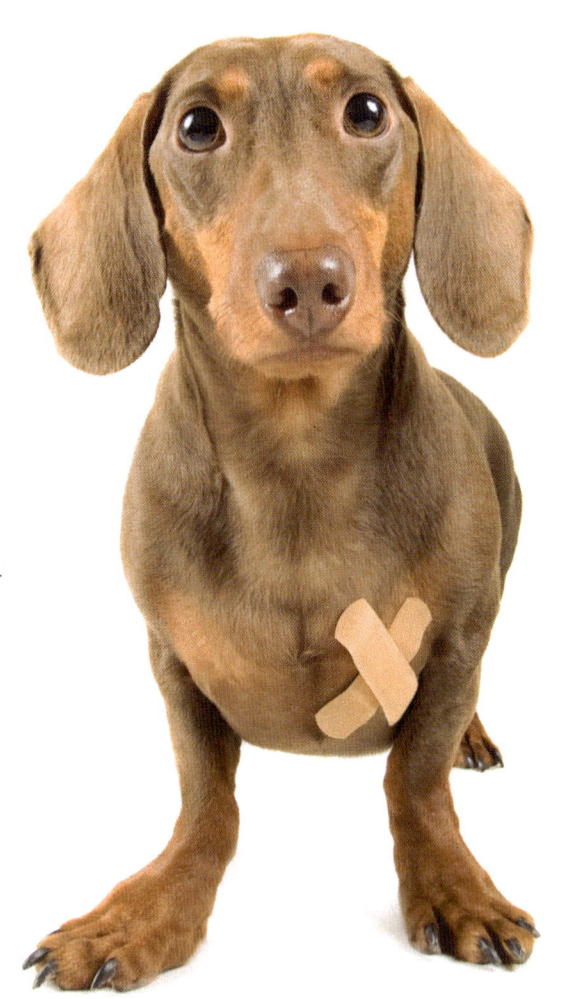

Happiness you will certainly again feel.

So hold on **tight** during your journey through grief.

As time passes,
you will feel happiness
and a sense of **relief**.

With age, **memories** of times shared with loved ones may fade.

But the great love that
we have for them grows **stronger** each day.

Grief is a healthy emotion, and it's healthy to embrace it.
By accepting loss, we clarify our values and the meaning of our lives.

Dean Koontz, Forever Odd
Published by Bantam Publishing, 2005.

THE PRICELESS GIFT OF LIFE

**When Sally, my beautiful, fit and healthy Mum
suddenly passed away, she was just 70 years young.
It was a deep shock to us all.**

**Luckily, she was a registered organ donor
and this selfless act improved the quality
and length of life for five people.**

With a warm smile and teary eyes, my Father said from the heart

*"Reading the letters of gratitude from the recipients of her organs was
enough to warm my heart and bring tears of joy in a time of grief."*

You too can leave a lasting legacy and improve the quality of life
for others. It's easy. Simply visit www.irodat.org then select
your country on the world map to find out the details
of your local organ donation organisation.

Get in contact with them, register to become an organ donor
and let your family know of your intentions.

"Giving the **ultimate gift of life** touches the hearts and lives of so many."

SPECIAL THANKS

To my family, in particular my amazing Dad of whom I'm so proud.

His positivity, friendliness and selfless acts of kindness towards others are highly admired, greatly appreciated and inspiring to those around him.

To my wonderful friends, who provided insightful feedback and shared great ideas from their particular areas of expertise – Sandra, Anne-Marie, Daniela, Lisa, Catherine and Aaron, Jeremy, April, Emma, Madeleine, Mary, Susana and Richard.

The ever resourceful Vanessa for recommending Dollar Photo Club and the breathtaking work of its talented worldwide network of photographers.

A huge thank you to my dear friend Cass of Cass James Design, whose graphic design expertise was pivotal in making the book come together in the most appealing and creative way.

A final heartfelt thank you to Merridy and Sally at DonateLife SA, for making the organ donation experience as pleasant as possible for my family, and for the ongoing kindness and support that you've shown towards my Dad.

All photographs are subject to copyright and have been used with permission from Dollar Photo Club. The photographers' names and pages that feature their photographs are listed below.

Eric Isselée   4, 6, 7, 8, 13, 20, 22, 23, 27, 29, 30, 36, 37, 42, 45, 56, 58, 64, 66, 67, 70, 73, 74, 75, 83, Back cover

Adrian Costea	35	inna_astakhova	76	oxilixo	87
Africa Studio	17, 46	jstaley4011	60	PASQ	In loving memory of Contents
aleksandr	44	Julia Remezova	47		
Anatolii	10, 43, 55	Kagenmi	39	phant	12
annette shaff	84	kasto	78	phspy	34
Bartkowski	15	Katrina Brown	81	Quasarphoto	62
biglama	21	Kavita	88	Sascha Burkard	53
blanche	38	khmel	28	Sergii Figurnyi	59
Bogdan Vasilescu	16	Kletr	61	Smileus	63
Cherry-Merry	85	Lars Christensen	89	speedphoto	79
Clivia	24	Mara Zemagaliete	71	Taalvi	31
cynoclub	25	Mat Hayward	51	tsepova	41
dimakp	40	mdorottya	54, 93	Vera Kuttelvaserova	2, 14, 52
duncanspila	26	Megan Lorenz	9, 86	Viorel Sima	11
eastmanphoto	82	Monika Wisniewska	57	Vladimir	50
fotomaster	65	Nikolai Tsvetkov	Front cover	Zharastudio	3, 72
iko	77	ots-photo	80		

Carolyn Jane Neill understands first-hand the shock of suddenly losing a loved one and the path of grief that follows.

Two years ago, her Mum unexpectedly passed away and her journey through grief began.

Like most of us, she jumped online to learn as much as she could about the grieving process. This helped her realise that what she was going through was natural and in time it would ease. Since, she has supported friends and colleagues faced with loss.

She is passionate about sharing her knowledge and experience to help those working through grief. She believes sharing 'Comfort for the Grieving Soul' is the perfect and practical way to show you care.

Carolyn is a communications professional consulting in Melbourne Australia. She has a Masters in Communication Management and enjoys helping people smoothly transition through life's many changes.

My thoughts...

Things that I enjoy doing that make me happy…

Made in the USA
Charleston, SC
27 June 2015